FOR MY EXTRAORDINARY FRIEND
SARA WRIGHT, WHOM I'D BE HONORED
TO RESCUE FROM A RUSHING CREEK,
A POND, THE WILLAMETTE RIVER,
OR EVEN A DEEP MUD PUDDLE.
—D.H.

TO ANDREA, MY BRIDE.

TO JACK, MY BOY.
(LEARN TO SWIM.)
—J.H.

✦✦✦✦✦✦✦✦✦✦✦✦✦✦✦✦✦✦✦✦✦✦✦✦ AUTHOR'S NOTE ✦✦✦✦✦✦✦✦✦✦✦✦✦✦✦✦✦✦✦✦✦✦✦✦

The events that are described in this story, so far as this author can determine from the accounts made by Abe Lincoln's neighbor Benjamin Austin Gollaher (1806–1898), did, in fact, take place—though whether Austin used a fishing pole or a sycamore branch in the defining moment of his life, I cannot verify (see *Best Lincoln Stories Tersely Told,* by J. E. Gallaher, 1898, as well as *The Boyhood of Abraham Lincoln, from the Spoken Narratives of Austin Gollaher,* by J. Rogers Gore, 1921).

This author has also uncovered evidence that Austin's gravestone in the Pleasant Grove Baptist Church Cemetery in LaRue County, Kentucky, identifies him as "Lincoln's Playmate"; a Kentucky Historical Society Marker (No. 827) also identifies Austin as "Lincoln's Playmate"; and, though the statement has been somewhat exaggerated elsewhere, in 1865 Abe Lincoln did apparently tell a Kentucky visitor, Dr. Jesse Rodman, that he would rather see Austin Gollaher "than any other man in Kentucky" (see J. William Weik's *The Real Lincoln: A Portrait,* 1922).

Abraham Lincoln's Boyhood Home at Knob Creek is part of the Abraham Lincoln Birthplace National Historic Site, which you can visit in person or on the Web at www.nps.gov/abli/index.htm.

✦✦

Published by Schwartz & Wade Books, an imprint of Random House Children's Books, a division of Random House, Inc., New York ✦ Text copyright © 2008 by Deborah Hopkinson ✦ Illustrations copyright © 2008 by John Hendrix ✦ All rights reserved. Schwartz & Wade Books and colophon are trademarks of Random House, Inc. ✦ Visit us on the Web! www.randomhouse.com/kids ✦ Educators and librarians, for a variety of teaching tools, visit us at www.randomhouse.com/teachers

Library of Congress Cataloging-in-Publication Data ✦ Hopkinson, Deborah. ✦ Abe Lincoln crosses a creek : a tall, thin tale (introducing his forgotten frontier friend) / Deborah Hopkinson ; illustrated by John Hendrix. — 1st ed. ✦ p. cm. ✦ Summary: In Knob Creek, Kentucky, in 1816, seven-year-old Abe Lincoln falls into a creek and is rescued by his best friend, Austin Gollaher. ✦ ISBN 978-0-375-83768-5 (hardcover) — ISBN 978-0-375-93768-2 (lib. bdg.) ✦ 1. Lincoln, Abraham, 1809–1865—Childhood and youth—Juvenile fiction. ✦ [1. Lincoln, Abraham, 1809–1865—Childhood and youth—Fiction. 2. Best friends—Fiction. 3. Friendship—Fiction.] I. Hendrix, John, ill. II. Title. ✦ PZ7.H778125Abe 2008 ✦ [E]—dc22 2007035149 ✦ The text of this book is set in Tribute. ✦ The illustrations are rendered in watercolor and pen-and-ink.

Book design by Rachael Cole

PRINTED IN CHINA
10 9 8 7 6 5 4 3 2 1
First Edition

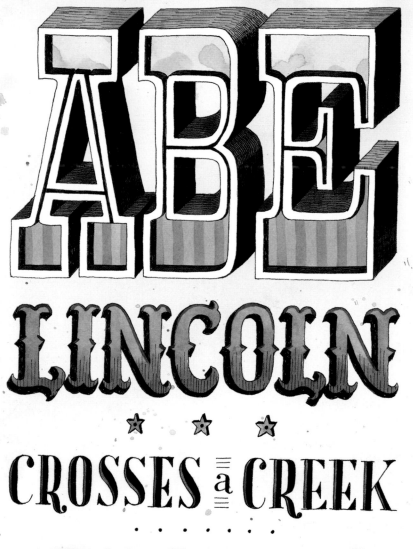

ABE LINCOLN

★ ★ ★

CROSSES a CREEK

. . . . . .

A TALL, THIN TALE

(Introducing His Forgotten Frontier Friend)

★ ★ ★ ★ ★ ★ ★ ★ ★ ★ ★ ★ ★ ★ ★ ★

DEBORAH HOPKINSON

PICTURES BY
JOHN HENDRIX

schwartz & wade books · new york

KENTUCKY · 1816

Now, here's an old tale of two boys who got themselves into more trouble than bear cubs in a candy store. I like it so well, I've asked my friend John to help out by drawing some pictures.

All stories have a time and place, and this one's no different. It happened on the other side of yesterday, before computers or cars, in the year 1816.

This green Kentucky valley is our place. Don't you feel like sticking your toes into that rushing water? That's Knob Creek.

Life was hard for many folks then, especially those in slavery. And in just a few years, all the cares of America would fall on the shoulders of one tall, thin man.

But in 1816 he's only seven. Here he is, fetching wood for his mother. All spring he's been helping his father plant corn and pumpkins.

Look, now he's stopping to watch a wagon rumble by.
I daresay you've guessed his name: Abraham Lincoln.
He'll grow up to become our sixteenth president.

There's another boy here, too, sitting on that
rock waiting for Abe. That's Benjamin Austin
Gollaher—Austin, for short.

Now, I can just hear you grumblin',

Well, Austin is Abe's first friend. He's three years older and as proud of Abe as a big brother.

"Abe's legs were long, his arms were long—why, even his ears were long!" Austin would say later. "And when it came to being smart, he was way yonder ahead of me."

All right, that's what we need to begin—a time, a place, and our characters: two boys named Austin and Abe.

Now, where were we? Oh, I know—Austin's just waved at his friend. Remember?

"Hullo there, Austin," Abe calls out. "Yesterday I saw some partridges over by Knob Creek. Let's go find them."

"Don't go too near the creek!" warns Abe's mama, Nancy. "It's been raining something fierce, and the water's high."

"We won't, ma'am," Austin and Abe chime together. Then they scurry directly there, wearing nothing but long homespun shirts.

Here's Knob Creek, its waters rushing through the limestone rock
into a dark, deep pool. I'd be scared to cross, wouldn't you?
But Abe points to the other side of the creek. "Let's go, Austin!
That's where I saw the partridges!"

Abe's only thinking about birds, not about the raging water before him. After all, he's just seven. Not a great leader yet, with the Union to save. Why, he's barely learned his letters!

"I don't know, Abe. The water's darn high."
Austin frowns. "And we can't swim."
"We can get across that log easy," says Abe,
with a plucky grin. "I dare you!"

"All right," replies Austin, gulping hard. Then, putting one foot in front of the other, he tiptoes across.

And then . . .

Let's all clap together: Austin made it!

Austin turns back to look for his friend. Uh-oh.
I sense trouble coming, don't you?

Abe takes a big breath and begins. His feet are
slippery. The log is slippery. He inches across.

Slowly . . . slowly . . .

Here comes the bit that's a mite scary—the part where if this were a movie, the music would get rumbly and you might cover your eyes. Abe looks down at the water, swirling and spinning.

Suddenly, he's dizzy.

ALAS!

ALACK!

Oh dear!

He's head over heels, and then—

HOLD ON

I want to be sure we get this right. Because maybe it didn't happen like that. I mean, would Abe and Austin really have WALKED across a log over that whirlpool? They weren't that foolish, were they?

ONE MINUTE!

No, I'm almost sure those boys would have *crawled*! So let's try again.

Now then. Austin stoops down, puts both hands on the log. He holds on tight. Bit by bit he pulls himself across to the other side.

Hooray! Austin is safe!

"Your turn, Abe," Austin says, squishing his toes in the mud.

Uh-oh. I'm afraid this isn't much better. Look—Abe's in trouble from the start. His stomach feels queasy. His head's all awhir. He gets halfway. He's stuck.

"Don't look down nor up nor sideways!" Austin hollers.
Can Abe even hear Austin above all the racket? John,
could you *please* stop painting that noisy water?

"Just look right at me and hold on tight," Austin yells louder.

But Abe can't help looking down. He loses his grip, and then . . .

ALAS! ALACK! Oh dear!

He's head over heels, and then—

SPLASH!

Wait. Where's Austin? Now, John, *don't* let him wander off to chase a partridge—not at the most important moment of his life!

Whew, there he is!

He must have been there all along. Because he was Austin, Abe's first friend, loyal and true till the day he died.

What's that you're saying? Abe's still in the water while I'm rambling on? His head went under again?

Wait, I'm trying to remember what happens next.

Hmmm, I'm pretty sure Austin *doesn't* say, "Don't worry, Abe. I'll save you, 'cause I know you're on earth for a great purpose."

And I don't expect Abe sputters back, "Stop yapping and help!"

No, I think Austin just leaps into action.

He pulls Abe out by his shirttail.

Or maybe he uses a sycamore branch—

or a fishing pole.

We'll let John decide which sketch to paint. For that's the thing about history—if you weren't there, you can't know for sure.

Abe's on land at last, but he looks almost dead. Austin pounds him until so much water pours out of his mouth, it about makes a lake.

For a long time Abe is still—as still as Austin's heart. At last Abe coughs. He opens his eyes and smiles up at his friend.

What a relief!

"I thought you were a goner," Austin says.

"I'm mighty grateful," Abe whispers, his throat raw from swallowing half the creek.

"Better not tell anyone," Austin says, "or we'll get a whipping."

"I won't. But I'll never forget it," Abe promises. "Not as long as I live."

Then they stretch out on the rocks and bake in the sun till they're dry.

We could end our tale here, two happy friends in the sunshine long ago. But I expect you want to know what happens next.

Not long after, the Lincolns move to Indiana.

In time, Abe goes on to the White House.

WHOA,

HOLD ON A MINUTE,

I'm afraid you've got it wrong: Austin wasn't there at the President's side.

Put him back by Knob Creek where he belongs, raising a family, riding a mule through the woods.

Telling stories of his first, great friend till he dies at the ripe old age of ninety-two, at long last, resting under a gravestone that reads LINCOLN'S PLAYMATE.

For the truth is, Abe and Austin never do meet again. But like he promised, Abe doesn't forget Austin. And one dark day in the midst of the Civil War (or so the story goes), Abe will be heard to say he'd rather see Austin Gollaher again than any other living man.

I like to think that's true, don't you?

Now we're coming to the last page. About all that's left is to remind you of the moral of our story: Listen to your mother and don't go near any swollen creeks.

What?

Oh, you don't think that's really the point? A mite weak, perhaps? Like Abe, a bit thin?

Then how about this: Remember Austin Gollaher, because what we do matters, even if we don't end up in history books.

Yes, let's remember Austin Gollaher, who, one day long ago, when no one else was there to see, saved Abe Lincoln's life.

And without Abraham Lincoln, where would we be?

But that's a story for another day. Because ours, at last, is done.